MW01028061

A Survivor's Guilt

by
April Goff

DEDICATIONS

This book is dedicated to anyone and everyone dealing with a trauma. You are not alone.

ACKNOWLEDGEMENTS

I would like to thank my friends and family, my parents especially, for always encouraging me and being there for me every step of the way.

Thank you to my mom, Sheryl Goff, for editing my book. Thank you to my dad, Iain Goff, for the image used on the cover.

I would like to thank every single individual that sent me a submission, whether it got printed into the book or not.

I would also like to thank everyone for supporting me on this journey. It's been a long one, and I'm so happy to have made it to this point with all of you.

Foreword

The author, who happens to be my daughter, has overcome many obstacles and hardships. I am proud of the woman she has become and the fact that what she has done here can help so many others who have unfortunately gone through similar traumas.

April was always known to be very outgoing. There was a time in April's young life as an early teenager when myself, husband and other family members suspected something was wrong. Unfortunately, I would have never thought it was childhood sexual abuse that she was going through. Looking back on that day when April came to me to today, there's no words to describe how immensely proud her father and I are.

During the last ten years, one of the major obstacles that April has overcome is severe anxiety with many different situations. She used to call me crying in the parking lot because she was too afraid to step foot into her university and it took many years for her to allow anyone to hug her again.

It brings us great pleasure that April allowed us to be a part of the process when she wrote this book.

Prologue

First of all, if you're reading this, I can only assume it is because you have gone through something similar to me and are trying to come to terms with it. Perhaps you want to feel you are not alone. I'd like to start off by saying, I am so proud of you for making it this far. Yes, this is corny, but I wanted you to hear this from someone.

For the most part, society likes to portray being a rape or sexual abuse survivor as this 'beautifully' tragic experience. There's a whole lot of focus on what society has deemed the 'good survivor,' or the 'quiet survivor.'

This survivor trope, shown in a lot of popular media usually has a survivor dealing with some sort of trauma. Throughout the story, we follow their struggle to process and come to terms with what they have been through. In the end, this survivor overcomes it all. They find that their trauma experience changed them for the better.

While it may be the goal for some survivors, and may be the outcome, this overall story isn't realistic. Trauma is messy. A lot of survivors never stop the healing process. The rape or sexual abuse may have taken place a long time ago. The person responsible may not be physically hurting you anymore. That doesn't mean it's over. For some, it's a never ending battle in their minds. It may always be a part of you.

Every survivor is different. Psychologists write books about trauma. There are many self-help books. They research for hours on end to obtain accurate information. No matter how well they research, or how much information they cram into a book, it will never apply to all survivors. While things in my book may not apply to all survivors, the overall message does. This message is that you are worthy and you are valid.

This book is meant to show the messy parts. It's meant to show you that while we may have dealt with different things, what each of us went through is real and valid. You aren't alone. If you aren't what society thinks is 'beautifully tragic' or a 'good survivor' then that's okay. Very few truly are. It's meant to get into the raw, hidden parts that are seldom spoken of and leave survivors feeling alone. Please note that this book is based a lot on my own personal circumstances, and therefore, mostly touches on childhood sexual abuse and rape. I believe in the validity of all trauma, but not having experienced it all means I won't be able to touch on the specific effects other trauma can have. This does not mean I think any trauma is more or less important. It just means that I feel I only have the right to speak on what I have experienced myself.

This book isn't based on statistics, or research. It's based on my view and experience as a survivor. I am not a licensed professional, but I am someone that has survived something horrific and I want to share my experience with you. Please don't take anything I write in here as medical advice. This book is meant to show you that you are not alone and give a voice to many survivors that deserve to be heard.

Telling my story is important because it not only helps me face my own feelings, but also lets other survivors know that it's okay to talk about it. My hope is that with this book, it helps pave the way for other survivors. I hope it helps them find their voices.

At the end of each chapter, there will be submissions from other trauma survivors sharing their experiences. Credit has been given word for word as they asked. Some contributors shared their names. In some cases, they only wanted to share their gender and age. A lot chose to remain anonymous.

Please be aware, before you proceed, that

most of the content of this book could be extremely triggering. Please only read if you feel comfortable to do so, and take breaks as needed. Most importantly, be safe and remember that you are valid.

Chapter 1

The Truth about Healing

"It's two am and you're keeping me awake.
The memory of your touch haunts me.
And I'm sure you're sleeping just fine."

I'm traumatized. There's no 'pretty' or 'neat' way of putting it. I went through something horrific. I deal with trauma every single day.

It's been over ten years since my initial trauma. There have been a couple isolated events as I got older, but for the most part, it's all about the trauma I endured growing up. There's no quick fix. There are periods of time I'll feel I'm doing good. These periods of time can range from days to even months. It'll feel like it's over. It'll feel like I've healed. Then out of nowhere, it hits me. I'm back there all over again. The healing never stops for me. There are bad days. There are good days.

Despite my knowledge of how healing works, I still find myself let down when I fall again. Every time I'm happy, I think, "This is it! I've finally done it. I've moved on." Unfortunately, I'm usually met with a crash. I hit a wall and then the pain starts all over again. It feels like the worst pain of my life every time it happens. I have to constantly remind myself I've gotten through it before and I can do it again. I feel like I've failed. I feel like I let myself down. It takes me awhile to convince myself that this is false.

I'm not weak or a failure. I'm an individual who has had to experience an awful event, and a part of it will always linger with me. This does not mean that healing is an impossibility. It just simply means that healing doesn't happen in straight, upward line. It sounds cliché, but that doesn't mean it's not true. The most accurate way I can think to describe it is: Healing is a rollercoaster.

It's completely normal for you to feel "over it". It's completely normal for it to feel like the trauma is happening all over again. A lot of people feel they've taken steps back. I don't like the metaphor. You aren't "going backwards." We're coming back to that metaphor. You're riding a rollercoaster that you can't get off of, that never stops. In a lot of cases, it's one of the wooden ones that scares you into thinking it's going to break and kill you at any given moment.

It's not your fault. There's no easy way to get

back on solid footing. It's probably very likely that you are doing everything you can to get better, but there is still no quick way off the ride. The thing that I want you to remember is that you are not on the ride alone. We're all with you. Perhaps at different points on it, but still there with you. Some of us are screaming. Others might be crying. Possibly getting sick… Maybe not even noticing we're on the ride because we've learned to drown it out. It's conceivable that some of us are, at the moment, enjoying it. The bottom line is that you aren't alone.

Eventually, you'll find the rollercoaster is smoother. It'll slow down. You won't be able to get off of it, but you'll be able to breathe easier. It'll be like the kiddie rollercoaster. In my opinion, this is healing. The trauma never leaves you, but you learn to handle it in a way that doesn't disrupt your life the way it used to. The twists, turns and ups and downs will still be there. You'll still drop to come back up. However, it'll be manageable. I've never heard of anyone getting off of the rollercoaster completely. And that's okay. The trauma never goes away, but you'll gradually gain more control. The noise of the trauma will fade in your head, locked away in a room where the knocking grows quieter.

Sometimes, the knocking will be abrupt and your unwanted visitor will find its way back into your life. That's okay. You'll get quicker at slamming the door in its face time and time again.

I'm sure that you've noticed I use a lot of metaphors. For myself, I find them easier. I find it easier to personify my trauma as an unwelcome visitor, and my healing as a ride I can't escape. Visualizing it helps me, and I'm hopeful it'll bring aid to you as well.

The reality is that I am on that rollercoaster still. I spend a lot more time on the upward climb, but I do still drop. I think I always will, it's just that it'll get easier in time.

When it gets bad again, I can hear the sound of his footsteps coming down the hallway. The fear I'd feel in my chest as I felt him get closer. I knew what was coming, and I was helpless to stop it. From the first time, I quickly learned that saying 'please, don't' would not make it stop. I still begged every time.

I'm older now. More capable of protecting myself. During these flashbacks, I'm still a child. Filled with terror. Sometimes, it happens during everyday things and I can continue on with whatever task I'm working on. My hands may shake, but I can still appear functional to those around me.

There are times when it consumes me. Like

when I'm alone when I hear it. Like when it's night when I remember. I can't figure out where I am. It feels like I'm back there and I can feel his hands. It's as if I am being violated all over me again. It feels like all the events in my life after that point don't exist. I don't know how old I am. I don't know that I'm safe. I don't know that he's nowhere near me and can't hurt me anymore.

During the abuse as a child, I learned to go somewhere else in my head. I'll still rely on this learned reaction to events in my life, to this day. Whether it's something like a break up, or just a bad day. I've mastered the ability to revert inside, and go somewhere else, like it isn't happening. It's something I'm still struggling to unlearn.

Healing is a different process for everyone, and everyone reacts differently. It's very common for people to talk about rape or sexual abuse survivors becoming sex repulsed. It's accepted, and it's assumed that it's the 'normal' reaction.

I'm here to tell you there is no normal reaction. Some survivors, yes, they become sex repulsed and can't stand any sort of physical contact. That is not, however, the only common reaction. There are those that react on the opposite end and become hypersexual. There are also those that fluctuate between the two or even happen to be both

5

at the same time.

I believe the latter, the hypersexuality, needs to be understood and talked about more as a lot of survivors feel shame regarding it. After talking to numerous survivors, I've found that, a lot of individuals admit to being hypersexual. In all honesty, very few people told me that they were sex-repulsed without experiencing any form of hypersexuality as well. I believe this is why it is crucial to talk about. Over half of the people who submitted their experiences did so anonymously. The shame and stigma surrounding hypersexuality is a problem. No one should feel ashamed or silenced. Yes, people are sex-repulsed. Yes, it is important to talk about. However, it's important to talk about hypersexuality as well because individuals who experience it, more often than not, feel like something is wrong with them because they don't fit in with the 'norms' dictated by society. The thing I've heard the most is that a lot of survivors go back and forth. That is okay. You aren't alone. People might not talk about it, but I am hoping in time it is discussed more.

Another thing pushed on survivors by society is the idea that you need to forgive your rapist or abuser and let go of your anger at them. I believe for some people, forgiveness may be necessary to their healing, but I do not believe it is the same for everyone. Everyone is unique and requires different things in their healing. You'd think that would be straight forward. A lot of people like to interject and push "forgiveness" on us. They'll even try and sugarcoat it with "forgive them for yourself." If forgiving them does give you some peace, then I'm all for it. It's more often though that I find survivors overwhelmed with guilt because they can't forgive or don't want to. They feel like they've failed or they're not a good person.

Pushing survivors to forgive may make them feel invalid or frustrated with themselves because they aren't in that place yet. Some survivors may never get to that place. I believe that's okay.

I can't speak for anyone else but when I felt anger towards my abuser it was a sign of my own healing. I'd felt angry at myself for so long and blamed myself. This anger I felt towards him was a significant step for me. I was now putting the blame on the person responsible instead of myself.

A lot of people are really against anger, but anger isn't necessarily a bad thing. Anger can push you to do things that need to be done. Anger can drive you to fight things that should be fought. Anger has been a huge part in many of the best changes in our history. Anger can be destructive, but it can also be productive. The key is harnessing that energy and not letting it be out of your control.

I do believe that in some cases, anger may consume someone and control their life. However, pushing someone to let go of it may make them feel bad or possibly focus that anger on themselves again. If you feel angry, please don't feel bad about it. Don't feel obligated to forgive. Take things one step at a time and try not to cave into the pressure from society or those around you. If you forgive them one day, that's okay. If you never get to that place, that's okay too.

Stigma seems to go both ways in the forgiveness part of trauma. Some think you're weak for forgiving, like you're saying what happened was okay. Some think you're wrong to not forgive. You are not weak if you forgive that person. It does not mean you're saying it was okay. It means that you're in a place where this is what you need, and ultimately, your healing is about you. The same is to be said about not forgiving. You're not a bad person. Try and remember that YOU are the priority in your healing.

Don't let others tell you the "right" way to heal. The only right way is whatever is right for you. It might seem confusing or overwhelming, but deep down, you know what you need. You'll figure it out. I promise.

As hard as it is, I believe it's necessary to find someone to talk to help you through the next step of your journey. If you do not feel safe talking to anyone you know, there are a lot of resources available that I encourage you to seek out. If you aren't comfortable talking to someone you know, there are hot-lines and online resources to start you off. Having someone to help you will lighten the burden. You do not need to carry the weight yourself.

The next part of this is admitting that yes, it happened and it is a big deal. I spent so long convincing myself that it was not a big deal. I believe this helped me to be in denial of the events so that I did not have to feel it. Acceptance, for me at least, was key to the beginning of the healing process.

In my opinion, it's important to get to the point when you realize what took place is terrifying. Saying "I was raped" or "I was abused" or even "I was assaulted" may be scary and difficult. You might choke on the words, but when you finally get them out, I believe you'll feel a weight being lifted. Whether you admit them to yourself or to a trusted individual, I believe that it is a critical step.

It's normal for survivors to try and downplay their experience by saying "it wasn't a big deal."

They'll rationalize to themselves that others have survived worse. What others have been through doesn't change what you experienced. Your pain is your pain. What you went through was real. It doesn't matter how "bad" it was. Or that it could have been worse. It should NEVER have happened to you. It was wrong. You are allowed to hurt over it, and yes, admit it IS a big deal.

When I was raped as an adult, I downplayed it too. "He could have hurt me more." "I went through so much worse as a child." This was denial. Eventually it came back on me, and it wasn't pretty when it did.

These next few paragraphs have been written in to me from different survivors.

One moment I am my present day self. The next I am about five or six years old, curled up on the floor, shaking so badly that my hands tremble and my teeth chatter. I'm terrified beyond belief and I can hardly breathe because I'm hyperventilating. I know what I'm remembering– a session of physical discipline from years ago. And the emotions I felt then (fear, betrayal, helplessness) are all echoing and amplifying until I can't contain them within my physical body. This lasts thirty to forty-five minutes, and I still tremble for hours afterwards until I finally fall asleep.

- *Anonymous*

The thing about healing after being raped is that every day it feels different. I can wake up one morning feeling empowered and like I have healed, and then I can crumble to the ground insisting that what she did to me was my fault in the blink of an eye. It cycles. I do this over and over, and I really don't know if I will ever be in an empowered, healing mood and stay there. But what I do know is that I manage to pick myself up time and time again. Each time I think about what happened to me and each time I talk about it, I get stronger. When I confronted my rapist, I ripped my power out of her hands with every word that spilled from my mouth. I may keep crumbling when I remember, but I will always stand back up, if for no other reason than to show her that I am more than what she made me feel like I am.

- *Emmett (18) trans guy*

I was attacked a little over a year ago. I recently started therapy and the healing process. I feel ashamed when my therapist talks about the times I've been raped. I am learning that even though I've been hurt, I can still get better

- *Anonymous*

After reading the submissions and the chapter, you can see that every survivor is different. I'm going to summarize it all for you again. It's important, and I want you to remember it. The ideals and norms that are enforced by society make matters worse. Survivors are often frustrated by the pressure to live up to society's expectations of them. The message I hope to convey is that it's okay. It's okay to not be the ideal survivor. It's okay if it's messy.

It's okay if you thought you were over it but it hits you all over again. It's okay to fall apart even after you thought you had it under control. You are not weak. Healing is messy. And there is no timeline for healing. It's okay to have bad days, even years after the last traumatic event. The fact that you're still pushing on means you're strong in my eyes.

Healing from trauma isn't pretty. It's not the beautiful breakdowns you see on film and TV. It can be ugly crying. The heart-wrenching sobs that leave you with snot coming out of your nose. It can even cause you to throw up. It's not pretty, and that's okay.

Please don't put pressure on yourself to be a 'good' or 'beautiful' survivor.

You are a survivor, and that's enough.

Chapter 2

Struggling with Feelings of Validity, Consent and Shame

I mentioned this struggle briefly in the previous chapter. It ties into feelings about how "it's not a big deal." That line of thinking is more than denial in some cases. A lot of it comes from feelings of validity or the lack of it. It's not uncommon for survivors to invalidate themselves.

They may think what happened to them "wasn't that bad" compared to things that happened to others. Some survivors may feel that their experience wasn't valid because they didn't fight back, or it wasn't violent. In some cases, survivors may invalidate their experience to try to deny what happened to them. They also may minimize it so they don't have to accept that it's a big deal, and that it's reasonable to have lasting trauma.

These feelings are normal, and as hard as it is, you need to remember that you are valid. What you went through, and how you feel about it is valid and okay.

I try to stay away from thoughts like "oh, this person had it worse than me. I have no right to be upset because their experience was clearly worse."

My mom always told me something that helped. She told me, "Your reality is your reality. No one else's. If it hurts you, it hurts. It's okay to feel."

Throughout the years, I've learned she is right. Whatever others experienced, what happened to you was still wrong.

For the longest time, I felt ashamed. I felt like because I didn't speak up when I was younger about what I was enduring, that I had no right to be upset. I felt like because I let it go on for years without speaking up that I wasn't valid. There was so much fear and worry. I felt like I had done something wrong. It took me years to go to my parents about what was happening to me. I was thirteen when I finally approached them.

I was so terrified that they wouldn't believe me, or if they did, that they would be angry at me. This wasn't the case. I approached my mom first. She let me speak and it took me a little bit to get the words out, but she waited patiently. The first thing she said to me was, "I believe you." The second thing she said was, "It's not your fault."

Those were the words I desperately needed to hear. I know a lot of people weren't as lucky as me when it came to having the support of their family, but I was. My mom went and spoke to my dad for me and he told me he believed me too.

Even though my mom and my dad validated me, I still struggle with these feelings to this day. I wonder if I'm still allowed to be upset or hurt by what happened. It's taken a long time, but I've come to the conclusion that yes. Yes I am still allowed to be upset. I'm allowed to be angry and hurt. The man responsible took away my childhood, and that still sits with me to this day despite the fact I am an adult.

What he did to me impacted how I would learn and cope with numerous events in my life. He, unfortunately, taught me to numb myself when things are too much to handle. I'm struggling, to this day, to not shut my emotions down the second things get rough. It was a coping mechanism back then, but I haven't quite mastered the art of feeling things the way I should.

I've come a long way in the healing process but the trauma does still affect me and I am learning that there is no set time line for healing.

There is an abundance of people that feel they are helping trauma survivors by telling them they need to "get over it." Perhaps they try and cover up that harsh statement and cushion it slightly. The overall message still leaves us beating ourselves up. This is because a lot of us already feel this way. In a lot of cases, and for me specifically, we already feel like we should be over it. I often feel it's a sign of my weakness that I'm not healed yet. Putting this sort of pressure on someone does little if anything to help them.

I'm here to tell you that whatever you feel is valid. It doesn't matter if it happened last week or fifty years ago. If it still hurts you, it still hurts you. Just because you are struggling doesn't mean you aren't healing or doing your best. The truth of the matter is, even if you do everything by the book, there's a very good chance your trauma will still affect you years later. I'm here to tell that it is okay. You are still valid even if you have bad days or the wound still seems fresh. Healing is a process, and it isn't a neat one. It's messy, and no matter how many books you read or how much help you seek, it'll be hard. Every person is different and there's no three, or five, or ten step program to heal from something like a traumatic experience. I know I already spoke about healing and timelines in the previous chapter, but I believe it's important. A lot of people feel because their trauma happened so long ago, their feelings aren't valid anymore because they should 'be over it'. That's simply not true. There is no specific amount of time which it "should" take to heal.

Usually when I find myself in that state of mind, where I feel I should be "over it" already, I stop and think to myself. Would I tell another survivor to simply "get over it?" I always reach the conclusion, that no, I would not. I would tell them to take as long as they need.

This leads me to my question, why do I expect myself to be different? Sometimes this helps, and sometimes it doesn't. I feel it's important for you to ask yourself, too. Would you tell another survivor to just "get over it?" Would you tell another survivor their feelings aren't valid? What would you tell your best friend? I'm assuming and hoping that you would not tell your friend to "get over it." You **would** tell them that they were valid and allowed to feel how they feel. Now, that being said, I want you to stop and think of yourself as that best friend. Yes, it's corny, but you deserve the same respect and understanding you would give that best friend. You have to remember it's been YOU all along. You've been the one consistently pulling yourself up every time you fall down. You've made it this far, and even if you had help along the way, in the end it was you who pulled you through.

I've also come across individuals that feel because they were in a relationship with the person, they have no right to call it rape or sexual abuse. Physical abuse is often talked about in relationships, but the sexual abuse part isn't. Rape and sexual abuse in a relationship can happen, and it is every bit as real and valid as it would be with a stranger. Dating someone isn't automatically consent. It doesn't matter if you've been dating them for a couple days or married to them for years, rape is rape. Being with someone doesn't automatically give them consent or rights to your body.

I suppose that might bring us to a question. What exactly is consent? I'm sure to many people, this question seems simple and straight forward. I've often heard the slogan "No means no." It's lately that it's been heard "Yes means yes." This is because it's finally being acknowledged that silence is not consent. However, this still doesn't cover the whole picture. I believe consent needs to be taught about more. It's a sad reality that a lot of people do not understand consent. This applies to both parties. The one asking for consent, and the one "giving" consent. The person asking may think it is okay to "convince" the person. Perhaps they think the person "wants" to say yes. The person "giving" consent may think they were not assaulted because they said yes when they were pushed into it. These are both wrong!

Here's a consent checklist to break it down:

These are questions both parties need to ask themselves.

Is this a "yes"? Is it freely given?
Freely given means that they haven't been pressured, threatened or guilted into saying yes. For example, this means that if you're their boss, they're not saying yes just to keep their job. If you're in a position of power over them, it's going to be extremely difficult to be sure their 'yes' is actually freely given – be extremely cautious. It also means that they aren't just saying yes to make you stop harassing them. Which also means, if someone says no and you keep asking until you get a yes... That is NOT consent.

Are they capable of consent?
Consent cannot be given when someone is incapacitated. This means, if they are passed out or under the influence of alcohol or drugs, they cannot consent. Keep in mind, children are never capable of consent to sex!

Do you have consent for the specific thing you're about to do?
Consent must be given for each action. Just because you receive consent to kiss someone, doesn't mean you have consent to grope them.

Did you get their consent this time?
Just because they've consented to this before doesn't automatically mean it's okay this time. Being in a relationship with someone doesn't automatically mean you have consent!

Do you still have their consent?
If someone changes their mind, you need to stop immediately.

Sometimes people decide that they want to use different standards of consent. This is especially common for people in relationships. Sometimes they'll decide that they don't need to say yes every time. Or maybe they'll decide that it's ok to start something when one or both people are drunk or asleep. This is okay as long as these things are established and agreed upon beforehand between all parties involved. The same rules about consent apply to making these new agreements, too. Someone who is too drunk to consent is too drunk to negotiate an alternative consent agreement. It's not okay to pressure someone into agreeing. And if they change their mind, the agreement stops.

A lot of struggles with validity come from confusion over consent. It doesn't matter what you were wearing, where you were, or how you reacted. You are valid. It doesn't matter what your gender is or your age. Rape, assault or sexual abuse can happen to anyone and it doesn't mean there's something wrong with you. Another thing I want to mention here is rapists and/or abusers aren't always males. It doesn't matter the gender of the person responsible, you are still valid. You are allowed to be traumatized, and anyone or anything that makes you feel weak is wrong.

The violence of rape or sexual abuse doesn't always involve physical force. Emotional coercion and other subtle forms of violence can also be a part of a rapist's strategy. Just because your rape wasn't bloody, or physically violent doesn't mean you aren't valid. I want you to know that if you froze, you're still valid. Many survivors freeze, myself included.

I remember thinking, "I will never let anything like that happen again," and "I'm older, stronger, smarter, more capable." I'd distance myself from my childhood trauma and have it in my head that I wasn't vulnerable anymore. That because I was older, I could defend myself. I carried this idea into a dangerous situation. I convinced myself I was fine. This situation was under my control. I was older now, I could prevent it even if the situation seemed to escalate. I thought, "That can't possibly happen again."

The truth is, it did. I froze and I had to endure another rape over ten years after I'd been raped for the first time. It took me a long time to accept that I wasn't at fault because I let myself believe I was in control, or because I froze. The fault is still that of my rapist. Even now, it's hard for me to admit it. I'm only doing so because I know there's others like me out there that feel they don't deserve to feel hurt or even angry. I want you to know that you aren't alone.

I struggle to admit I was raped in adulthood, and not just childhood. A lot of this has to do with the fact that there seemed to be a lot more blame put on me as an adult. When I finally got the courage to tell others what had taken place, some of the questions I was met with made me wonder momentarily if I was partially to blame.

"Were you drinking?" "What were you wearing?" "Did you lead him on?" "Why were you alone with him?"

The answers were, "No," "Sweatpants and a tshirt," "I told him that I wasn't interested in him before hanging out," and the last one, people seem to get stuck on, "Yes, I was alone with him, but I thought he was a friend."

One person seemed genuinely shocked at my answers, as if they were somehow hoping to have a way to argue I was at fault. For the record, even if I was drinking or met him completely naked, it would still be his fault for raping me. Even if I had expressed interest, that doesn't give anyone the right to my body.

This person, after getting over their initial shock, then voiced their opinion of, "Well, you shouldn't have been alone with him."

My response was simple: "Well, he shouldn't have raped me."

There's something I've left out and haven't told a single person because I know the judgment that typically follows what I'm about to tell you. He and I had flirted a bit, and discussed the possibility of having sex. I wasn't comfortable with it and told him so. There were several reasons, but a major one was that it brought forth too many traumatic memories. He laughed it off and agreed. He seemed to get it, so when he asked me to hang out again, I said "yes" to that. I'd thought we'd come to an understanding.

Once we were alone again, I felt uncomfortable. I told myself it was all in my head and I was just being paranoid. I didn't believe it was happening until it actually did, and once it started, I went somewhere else in my head. I told him again, just before we'd hung out, I didn't want to sleep with him. I was as clear as I could be, right before we met up.

When he started to touch me, I froze. I reverted back to the way I'd reacted when I was a child, and I went somewhere else. I didn't tell him no at this point. I'd told him no before I'd seen him. He knew he didn't have consent. My tears and the way I shook were ignored. He'd known previously my issues with trauma and I'm sure he had some idea that I was a vulnerable target.

Please be aware before proceeding that this next paragraph is likely very triggering as it is descriptive. Please, skip to the next paragraph if this isn't something you're ready to read. I've made the font in the next paragraph smaller so you can see what part you may want to skip. I'm only including this paragraph to show you that the absence of the word no does not mean what happened isn't rape.

I remember his hand on my leg, moving up my inner thigh. I pushed his hand away, and he laughed and put it back on me. This took place in my truck and one of my hands tried to reach for the door handle, but he stopped me. It's a blur, and I don't remember whether he removed my pants or whether I did. I just remember feeling his hand on my bare skin and there was nothing there to protect me from his touch anymore. I started to cry as he began to remove his pants. Once he'd removed them, I froze. I stopped moving, aside from the trembling. There was nothing in me anymore. I'd gone somewhere else in my head. I couldn't feel, move or even speak. A few moments of pleasure for him turned into a life time of pain for me.

As I said previously, I haven't told anyone this. This is my first time telling anyone the fact that I hadn't said no, and that I'd considered sleeping with him, before that. I'm only doing so because I want you all to know that no matter what, you're valid. I'm not a fan of "no means no" as an anti-rape slogan because it makes a lot of other survivors feel invalidated. Even if someone doesn't actually say no, that doesn't mean it isn't rape.

Whenever anyone asks me if I told him no, I say I had. In my mind, the fact that I told him no before we'd gotten together should be enough of a no. The fact that I tried to push him away or that I started to cry should be enough of a no. However, I know in a lot of people's eyes, the fact that I never spoke up during the act would make them doubt whether it was actually rape. I froze. That wasn't consent. It's taken me a long time to accept that I wasn't at fault. It took me a long time to accept that he had in fact raped me. He should have gotten my consent, or better yet, he shouldn't have touched me at all, because I'd told him that I didn't want to sleep with him. I had several reasons, including my past trauma. But the fact is, it doesn't matter what my reasons were. I could have not wanted to sleep with him simply because I didn't want to, with no further explanation – that would still be completely valid and would still make his actions rape.

I believe that people try and rationalize a rape into something else because they don't want to believe something so horrible could happen. People might argue that it was a simple misunderstanding, or that the raped person is trying to throw off their guilt and regret after the event. Rape does happen. No matter how much people may deny it. A huge part of victim blaming is that if you can find the victim at fault, you can convince yourself it would never happen to you. You wouldn't make leave yourself vulnerable the way they did. You wouldn't make the mistakes they did. I know it's scary to understand, but rape and assault don't work that way. You can do everything "right" to avoid assault, and have someone else do it to you anyway.

Another reason people victim blame is because they don't want to believe a rapist could do something so terrible. People who know the person accused, especially, often have a first instinct to defend the person accused. This is because to accept that a person is actually a rapist shatters their image of that person, who might be their brother, or aunt, or long time friend. It might cause a person to question their own judgement, and wonder, "Is it possible I didn't see what that person is capable of?" It can be much easier to deny the events ever happened, or deny they happened the way the accuser says they happened. Finding a way to blame the victim allows people to avoid accepting they might have been wrong about a person. No one's judgement of others is perfect. If you could always tell who was trustworthy and who wasn't, who would be a good friend or who would be a user, life would be much simpler. The fact that someone couldn't tell that their friend might be capable of rape doesn't make them less capable than most people, any more than the fact that you couldn't tell someone might assault you before it happened makes it your fault. We would all like to believe our judgement is perfect. This isn't realistic. The way victims are blamed for sexual assault in particular is further explained by the way sex is often stigmatized in our society and the way people don't always seem to understand consent. It seems like this should be no more true for assault and abuse than for other crimes, but we rarely hear, "Why were you carrying around so much money if you didn't want other people to have it?"

It's not uncommon for an individual that has suffered a traumatic experience to feel ashamed. They may not talk about it because they fear they are going to be judged. Most survivors blame themselves. Though there's no quick fix for this, it's important to try and remember that what another person did to you is not your fault. You didn't make the choice to have them assault you, they chose to assault you. They should feel ashamed, not you.

It doesn't help that there is a stigma attached to talking about rape or sexual abuse. This shouldn't be the case. This can contribute to survivors feeling ashamed. A lot of people have this idea that while rape does happen, it doesn't need to be talked about. People turn it into a secret thing which should be hidden away and buried. I think they're wrong. I think this just makes it harder for people to recover from assault and abuse. I think you should talk about it as often or as little as you need. You shouldn't feel ashamed in any way. You have done nothing wrong, and you have a right to talk about it. It might be easier for some people to never hear about abuse, but it isn't real and it doesn't help the people who actually went through things.

The next part of this chapter will include submissions from other individuals and their experiences.

What I experienced was emotional abuse, but I can't in good conscious call it that because every other person who's experienced a form of it has had it much worse. I often flip between being sure that it was abuse, and believing it was entirely my fault for not speaking up about things - but I never felt safe confronting my abuser because previously they would overreact to things I said. At this point all I've decided on is that my experience was quite toxic for me.

Anonymous

I told my mom how I was in a relationship for 3.5 months with a guy who raped and coerced me into sex, or would just rape me. She, along with former close friends of mine, said nobody would stay in a relationship if they were raped. Now my mom doesn't believe me when I tell her about the PTSD.

Liz

When I was twenty three I got back together with a girl I had dated in high school, the relationship was pretty good for the most part. One day her and I were fooling around on the bed and she expressed interest in having sex without a condom, I wanted to discuss it first and not rush things but she didn't want to talk and she pinned me down by my shoulders and proceeded to force me inside of her while I said stop and no. She continued to rape me until we both climaxed (I refuse to say orgasm), after she was done she left my place. I broke up with her about a month after it happened, at the time didn't think what had happened was rape because "it doesn't happen to men". Afterwards I began to drink a lot to try and kill the pain and I was too scared to seek mental help for the suffering it caused me. It took my two years to be able to come forward and seek help for it after having an alcohol related incident. I still carry the shame of being a male rape victim and to this day I don't see myself as the same person I was.

- *James*

I've struggled with the validity of my rape because I was in a relationship with the person and didn't fight back enough in my opinion and never yelled for their mom who I knew was in the room next door and let them violate me for years after... no wasn't allowed to be said and it took me four years to realize that the entire experience was valid...

- *Anonymous*

Just because they think you should be over it doesn't mean you're weak. You are not at fault for what someone else did to you, regardless of whether you fought back or not. Their actions are theirs alone. Please try to quit blaming yourself.

Everyone heals at different paces, and in different ways. And that's okay.

Chapter 3

How Trauma Can Sneak in Everyday Life

"I was a child.
You were a monster.
My innocence didn't stand a chance."

As I've stated before, just because the trauma itself isn't taking place any more, doesn't mean it's over. Trauma can and may affect someone years later, maybe even all their life. There isn't anything wrong with you if this is the case.

I find my trauma sneaks into my everyday life in ways I did not expect. I can be going about daily tasks and suddenly I feel his hands or his breath on my neck. Sometimes, there's an obvious trigger that I can associate with my response. Other times, I can't figure out what is going on.

Flashbacks aren't always a vivid re-experience of the event. Though this is the case at times.

Flashbacks can be scents, sounds or even smells. You could be sitting at your desk at work and suddenly you can hear his footsteps. It's also possible that you may not re-experience the flashback in the way it's often talked about. You may experience emotional flashbacks. These flashbacks, for me, often involve me going through the feelings of the event without seeing, smelling or hearing anything that took place back then. It doesn't make sense to me and suddenly I'm in a panic. My fight or flight response may kick in.

I'm going to backtrack a bit and talk about triggers. Triggers are talked about, but no one really talks about the triggers one might not think of. Usually, people talk about loud sounds such as the sound of firecrackers for war veterans. There are numerous things that trigger me, and many others, that individuals that have not gone through a trauma may not expect.

I want you to know this is okay. You aren't weak because a certain hat style may send you into a panic. It took me a long time to understand my triggers. One of them is saying 'I love you.' When I was younger, I was forced to say this to the man that molested me after he was finished. To this day, I choke on those words.

For the longest time, the smell of cigarette smoke made me uncomfortable because that's what he always smelled like. My brain had learned to associate the smell with him. There are times, over ten years later, that the sound of footsteps set me off. This is one of the most common sounds my brain links to my abuse. The sound of his steps approaching me as I tried to sleep and sometimes, when I hear that sound, it's like I'm on that couch again waiting for whatever he has in store.

When it comes to my most recent traumatic event, it's my vehicle that causes the panic sometimes. The rape took place in my truck, and there are times when I'm sitting in it, I can feel his hands again. For me, it usually comes back to the hands. The thing that led to the final event. The fear and anticipation of what was to come and the helplessness I felt to stop it. I've heard a lot of other survivors talk about the feeling of hands as well.

It's hard to not shut down when something triggers me. My immediate response is to go non-verbal, but usually I'm in a place where this isn't an option. I force myself to act like I'm fine but sometimes, the numbness still kicks in. Out of nowhere, I find myself in this emotional fog where nothing feels real and I'm going through the motions just trying to get through the day.

My goal with this chapter connects back with chapter one and how healing may never stop. There is nothing wrong with you because your trauma is still a part of your life. You aren't weak because there are days you struggle more.

Trauma can affect any number of things including your ability to set boundaries and your personal relationships. It's become a cliché in some stories and popular media about survivors having trust issues, which has merit, as this is the case for a lot of survivors. The other part that isn't normally talked about as much is how it can go the opposite way as well. Your trauma can cause you to latch on and trust someone too much, and in some cases, someone that doesn't deserve that trust.

It is not uncommon for survivors of childhood abuse to find themselves in an abusive relationship later on. It, unfortunately, seems to be true that survivors of any sort of trauma may be more vulnerable to another trauma later down the road.

While not healthy, some survivors even seek out dangerous and destructive relationships. This may happen for any number of reasons, including, but not limited to: feeling like they deserve the abuse, feeling like it's normal or it may even be them trying to find some semblance of control.

I'm not proud of it, but I have put myself into dangerous situations to try and prove to myself that I could get out of those situations and change my outcome.

I would never condone this unhealthy coping mechanism, but I do want you to know that if this is a coping mechanism that you use, I'm not judging. You shouldn't be judged and you aren't wrong or dirty because you feel that way. I hope that one day you are no longer in that place.

I was still in elementary school when the abuse started. As a child, my understanding of the world was still forming. The abuse has shaped who I am, and it's taken a lot of therapy and time for me to try and get it under control.

It's affected my personal relationships, my job and an abundance of other things as well. I believe the molestation as a child has warped how I view the world.

I always had a lot of anxiety. I always just thought of it as that. Anxiety. It never occurred to me until I started therapy that there was a reason for this anxiety. I was always in denial. I always said that what happened as a child didn't affect me. I was over it.

I wasn't over it though. I had no idea how much the trauma was affecting me. From the self-sabotaging to destroying relationships on purpose when people got too close, my trauma was sneaking through in my everyday life. It's taken me a long time to accept this part of myself and realize that it's okay. It's okay that I'm not 'over' my trauma. Maybe I never get 'over' it. However, I am learning to handle it. I'm learning to live with it.

As in the previous chapters, here are a few submissions from other survivors that want to be heard.

I always get weird looks from other people when I take forever to sit down at the table with them. Nobody realizes that a simple "sit down" is my worst trigger and causes me to tremble with fear. Nobody sees how these two words remind me of the time my parents would say them, make me sit down at the dining table and then yell at me for hours straight.

- Kellie, 18, Austria, finally working on becoming happy after moving out.

I deal with getting triggered nearly every day. Two of my main triggers are alcohol and sex, and in high school, it's nearly impossible to avoid conversations about both of these. Nobody knows this though. When I'm triggered, I freeze up and won't do or say anything for a while. I can do nothing but sit in silent fear.

Nobody ever notices. I'm not sure if I'm grateful for this, or hurt by it. I still don't know how to cope with being triggered so often.

-   Anonymous female (16)

Red Chevy pickup trucks are very common in the south. So are tallish light haired men. Whenever I leave my house I am surprised at how often they cross my path. These are both things that send me into a panic. My mind gets flooded. Is that him? Did he find me? Is he really here?
At some point, years after what happened to me, I found out it was easier to just stay inside, away from all the reminders. I dropped out of college, decided not to get a job, stopped hanging out with friends, all so I wouldn't have to be reminded. He hurt me years ago now, but he's still taking away my future.

-   Graham

In my case, doors are somewhat of a trigger sometimes. Like if someone opens my bedroom door without knocking, when I hear someone knocking on the door, when I hear someone unlocking the door, etc. My mom was abusive when she got home and I hadn't cleaned the way she wanted me to. During some time, she wouldn't open the door, she made me do it and say she wasn't home. Later I found out it was because my dad owed money to drug dealers and they were threatening to hurt us. Also my bedroom door didn't even close properly, I asked my mom for a lock and she said no. My dad snuck into my room every morning and molested me for some time. So if I hear knocking, someone opening a door, unlocking a door, etc, I get really scared and tend to freeze.

- *Anonymous*

Whatever your trigger, you aren't weak for feeling that way. There may even be things that trigger you that you haven't quite figured out yet. I know I've said it a lot, but it doesn't make you weak to have triggers. You went through something traumatic, and your brain is still trying to make sense of it.

Chapter 4

Anger and Forgiveness

Before I get into this chapter, I'm going to start off by saying you aren't wrong whether you choose to forgive or not. I've touched on this previously, but the topic is important and I feel deserves some more depth.

For some survivors, forgiveness may be fundamental in their healing but this doesn't exclusively mean that you have to forgive in order to heal. Society often suggests that an individual must forgive their abuser in order to heal. I believe this contributes to the 'quiet' survivor stereotype that is pushed on us.

Simply put, I'm not a fan of telling someone they have to forgive their abuser. While some may find comfort or peace in doing so, it isn't for everyone. If it's something an individual chooses to do, it should be on their own time and not something they're pushed into.

40

Forgiveness, for some, may mean letting go. There's nothing wrong with that. I'm also here to tell you that you don't have to forgive your abuser.

It doesn't matter if they are mentally ill, blood related, or were abused themselves. There is no reason you have to forgive someone. If you are going to forgive your abuser, please do so for yourself. You're what matters in all this. A lot of survivors may feel pressured because their abuser has apologized to them. You don't owe them anything, even if this is the case. You do not know them anything, even if they have genuinely changed for the better.

I'm not here to tell you not to forgive. I believe that's up to you. I'm here to tell you that it's okay one way or the other whether you choose to forgive or not. While it may help some heal, for others it doesn't.

I know there are some survivors that feel they are being judged for forgiving. Forgiving someone does not mean that you are saying what they did was okay. I also know there are those that feel pressured by family or society to forgive their abuser, especially if there are other things at play like relation or mental illness.

In my personal experience, I have not forgiven my abuser. I was a child when I was molested and it went on for years. He used to tell me if I told my parents they wouldn't love me anymore. Which was a manipulation he used because he knew what he was doing was wrong. Forgiveness isn't in the cards for me. At least not at this time. Maybe there comes a point in the future where I do forgive him. Perhaps I never forgive him. Either way, it's okay. I don't owe him anything. Whatever I do, it's going to be for me.

I have too much anger at him to forgive him. Honestly, the anger I feel at him is a step for me in the right direction. I spent a long time blaming myself and being angry at myself. The fact that I've put that anger on the person responsible means, for me, that I've stopped blaming myself.

The only person at fault for what happened to me was the man that did it. That being said, while I believe it's okay for survivors to be angry, I know it can consume you. I only speak from my personal experience.

I let my anger consume me for the longest time. While I believe that I'm allowed to be angry at him, this anger I felt for him was getting in the way of my life. All of my energy was put into hating and being angry with him. It took away from other things, and became my focus.

I'm still angry, but it doesn't consume me anymore. He's not every thought in my life. He isn't my focus. I don't let my anger for him ruin me. I'm only bringing this up because I know society has this idea of the quiet, kind and 'good' survivor. They don't think survivors should be angry and that it's a waste of energy.

I believe being angry can take your energy, and take away from the life you deserve, but I also believe a survivor has a right to be angry. They were the ones violated. They were the ones that had to endure the helplessness and pain. I don't think anyone has the right to tell a survivor they cannot be angry or shouldn't be.

I am angry, and I probably will be for a long time. I was a child and this man was someone trusted to look after me. What he did to me took away from the childhood I deserved to have and still sits with me to this day.

I want to touch on one more thing before we get into the submissions portion of the chapter. What a lot of survivors struggle with is feeling like they don't have the right to be angry. For some, this comes from a struggle to feel valid. They feel what happened wasn't that bad, and they don't have the right. Some survivors feel they aren't allowed to be angry because the person responsible was mentally ill. Another reason, something I haven't touched yet on in this book, is child on child sexual abuse (cocsa). The person responsible didn't realize what they were doing was wrong and this can leave a cocsa survivor feeling confused because they aren't sure whether they can feel angry.

I know it's confusing, but I firmly believe, a survivor always has the right to feel angry. They're allowed to feel however they feel, even if the person didn't realize what they were doing was wrong. What you went through was real and you are valid.

You are within your rights to feel angry. The part that matters most is what you do with that anger.

Here's a few submissions from other survivors and their experience with anger and/or forgiveness.

Every time my mother abused me, she would force me to apologize for 'making' her do it. Then she would apologize, too, and she would make me tell her I forgave her. If I showed any hint of anger or pain after that, I was punished with more abuse. Forgiveness is not positive for me, not after it was weaponized against me as yet another way to remove my agency and deter my resistance. I've found strength and healing in my anger. It's a way of reclaiming myself and rejecting the false narrative of my life she forced on me. It's been a powerful force in my recovery from PTSD. Because anger doesn't have to be destructive. Anger is what motivates me to do better than my abusers, help others, and spread goodness in this messed-up world wherever I can. Because what happened to me, to us, wasn't fair, there's so much that isn't fair, and I'll be damned if I don't do anything about it.

- *Anonymous*

I wanted to say- forgiveness does not equal healing
People say that in order to heal, you have to forgive your abuser.
Not true.
If anything one of the things I've seen about abuse that struck me most was that in all reality, being angry at your abuser means you're healing. It means you blame them, instead of yourself. You know it's not your fault and you know you have every right to be angry and every right to feel everything that your abuser made sure you couldn't. Learning and realizing that it's okay to feel, and it's okay to feel loudly and fully, and it's okay say "this person hurt me" was HUGE for me. Learning that it's okay to be angry about it because my personhood and the pain she caused me are worth being angry over-
Has been one of the biggest steps in my journey so far.

- *Skylar (16) trans male*

45

I haven't forgiven my rapist and I doubt I ever will. To me, recovery was about forgiving myself, and allowing myself to be angry with him. First after the rape, I couldn't feel mad at him, because I cared too much about him. Heck, I actually liked him. I was angry at myself instead, for not stopping him or fighting back enough. Finally allowing myself to feel angry for what he did and forgive myself (because I know I did nothing wrong) helped me so much.

- *Emelie Herlin*

As it's been pointed out, it's okay to feel angry. It's okay to forgive and it's okay not to forgive.

However, there is one person that I hope you forgive. There is one person that deserves your forgiveness. And that's YOU. If you're one of the few that doesn't blame yourself for what happened then that's great and I am so happy for you.

I don't believe anyone should blame themselves, but the unfortunate reality is that many do. Whatever the circumstances, it wasn't your fault, and it's time to forgive yourself. You deserve the peace that comes with that. You are not at fault. You are not to blame. You did not deserve what happened to you. If you aren't in that place yet, then that's okay, but I hope one day you realize this.

I hope you can forgive yourself.

Chapter 5

Internalizing the Struggle

There's been a chapter on anger and forgiveness, and we've touched on a few other points. In general, this entire book is about how trauma can affect you, however, this chapter is going to get into some of the darker parts.

Please be aware this chapter talks about self-harm and suicide, and if this is something you aren't ready to read, then please don't force yourself. This also talks about personal experience, so it may be a bit descriptive.

Trauma survivors react to their trauma in a lot of different ways. There isn't a rule book, and it's different for everyone.

Some people, like myself, may numb themselves. They may tell themselves it's not a big deal. It doesn't bother them. In my case, this meant I acted out in a lot of different ways and didn't fully understand why.

I was 12 when I started hurting myself. I didn't even know why I was doing it, not really. It started when I was in the bath one night. This was the last year of the abuse at this point. I was older now and around him a lot less. I'm not sure why, but I took the razor across my wrist. There was a relief. It made me feel free. It became an addiction.

I cut myself on and off until I was 22. While it's been a couple years, the scars are still there, and they're a permanent reminder.

I was also 12 when I tried to kill myself by overdosing on any and all pills I could find in my house. My parents didn't understand, and they couldn't, because I hadn't told them what was going on.

I was 13 when I finally told them, over a year after my abuser had left. They asked if I wanted to see someone, and I told them no. Even now, I appreciate that they didn't force me to. I wasn't ready to admit it to myself or accept it yet. I made the decision to see someone when I was 16 and she helped me explore a lot of what was going on. Even still, I was reluctant to accept what had happened to me.

She'd always bring up my trauma and I'd dismiss it. I'd tell her that it had nothing to do with why I did the things I did. In all honesty, she was right. I spent so much time denying it that by the time I started to deal with it, I was an adult. The man didn't just take my childhood, it took away my teenage years as well.

I was placed into the psychiatric ward three different times for suicide attempts. I would, or so I thought, have it all under control and then have an outburst of emotion that I couldn't get under control. In my panic and impulse, I'd try and end my life.

It wasn't until I was 21 when I finally admitted I wasn't doing as well as I thought. It was then that I went back to the police and told them what I'd left out years ago. This was a huge step for me. My hands still shook when I went into the details. I still choked on the words. But admitting it to myself, and out loud to someone else, left me feeling like a weight had been lifted from me.

To this day, I have a hard time saying I was raped. That I was molested and sexually abused. Sometimes, I still try and act like it isn't a big deal and it doesn't do me any favours. I downplay it to try and deal, but it always comes back in the end.

When I was raped as an adult, despite everything I'd learned, I buried it again. I parked on the side of the road for a couple hours, and then went home. I didn't even bother cleaning myself, I went to sleep. When I woke up, I'd forgotten it happened, until I felt the aches and saw the marks. I threw up, and sat in the shower for well over a half hour desperately trying to feel clean.

That's something a lot of survivors experience. A feeling of dirtiness. Some of us scrub and scrub but no matter what we do, we never feel clean. I want you to know that if that applies to you, you aren't dirty. I know just reading that won't fix anything, but I want you to tell yourself that. Tell yourself that you aren't dirty. You didn't do anything wrong. Tell yourself that every day, because it's true, and I hope one day you believe it.

Once I got out of the shower, I got dressed, and went to work and went on with my day and life like it hadn't happened. It felt like a dream. It didn't feel real.

People noticed I seemed a bit off, despite the fact that I thought I was doing a great job at hiding it. I told them I was tired. They believed me.

My best friend at the time figured it out on his own what had happened. I didn't tell him everything. I didn't tell him that I'd slept with the guy before because I felt he wouldn't think my rape was valid if he knew that.

We talked about it. We cried. We talked about it until I couldn't anymore and that was it. I felt like I'd faced my trauma and healed.

I moved on. Or so I thought. I hadn't faced it. Not fully. It still haunted me. I began to have angry outbursts, or hysterical ones for seemingly no reason.

I lashed out and sabotaged relationships and I didn't even realize what I was doing. They were self-destructive behaviours, and I thought because I'd experienced trauma as a child that I had it under control.

I rationalized it. I told myself that I went through years of sexual abuse and molestation, I wasn't going to be brought down by one more event. I told myself that I'd been through so much worse and that this was nothing.

I'm telling you this because I know there are others like me out there. And I want to tell you that it's okay. It's okay to feel it. It's okay to admit it was a big deal. It's okay to be upset, even if you think you've survived worse or someone else has. What happened was awful and you shouldn't compare it.

I lost my best friend because I didn't deal with my trauma the way I should have. I buried it, but parts of it came out. I began to act out the way I had before.

I kept telling myself I had it under control, but I didn't. That's one of the scariest parts for me. Not being in control. Every time I did something irrationally, I told my best friend, family and myself that I had it under control. It was fine. I was fine. I **wasn't** fine though. I was spiraling out of control and no one could help me because I was in denial. I was lying to myself and everyone around me because I thought it was best. I thought it wasn't a big deal and I thought was overreacting by still being upset about the rape a few months down the road.

I think to myself now, would I ever tell another survivor that they were overreacting for being upset about being raped or abused months later? The answer is no, of course not. I'd tell them they were allowed to feel how they felt for however long they needed. I've decided I owe myself that same respect and understanding. Don't tell yourself something you wouldn't tell another survivor. I know I've brought this up before but it's important.

My main point is, many survivors internalize the struggle because they don't want to bother anyone. That was my problem. I didn't want to inconvenience anyone, and in the end, I made it worse for them but most importantly, I made it worse for myself.

You can only bury it for so long, and it's scary, but you have to try not to hide from it. Otherwise, it'll sneak up on you when you least expect it.

Here are a few submissions from other survivors and the different ways they may internalize the struggle.

When I was dealing with the height of my abuse I fell into a bad depression. I was ashamed that I was depressed, because my dad had told me depression was weakness. In order to prove to myself that I wasn't, I made a list of things that I knew depression was. Then I told myself that so long as I never did anything on that list I wasn't depressed.

My list included skipping school and cutting myself and contemplating suicide. I refused to recognize my obvious symptoms like feeling that all of my emotions were fake, being constantly exhausted, insomnia, not eating, a lack of interest in everything. I refused to acknowledge my depression at all.

In the end that list prevented me from getting help for my depression for 7 years. It was only once I broke the rule about contemplating suicide that I realized I needed help.

- *Kaitlyn, 23, Colorado*

Okay, so... this is the first time I have ever admitted this but... I was raped. It was by a girl, two years younger than I was. I was born female. She didn't really respect that I identified as male. The entire relationship was toxic. The one day she came to my house she manipulated me into having sex with her. I don't remember consenting, I remember trying to go to sleep and nearly falling asleep until she woke me up by starting things. It was one sided, she did stuff to me and that was it. Afterwards I felt incredibly guilty. She bragged about being the one to take my virginity, I didn't even want to admit it had happened. I internalized everything. I buried thoughts of her. I pretended that nothing had happened between us. I never thought about that night until years later and only now are the feelings that should have hit when it happened hitting me now. Only now when I'm admitting things I hardly dared to think about back then are the buried feelings coming up to haunt my waking days as I agonize over this scenario.

-   *Septimus, age 18, trans boy*

Trauma can change you as much as you wish it wouldn't. It changes the way you view the world and it can change the way you interpret everything. It can leave you feeling stressed or pressured to go back to that person you were before the trauma.

It's okay to stop. It's okay to stop trying to be who you were before the trauma. It's okay if it's changed you. It's okay if you're different. You don't have to do what society says and 'come out better.' Maybe you're just different, not better or worse, just different and that's okay. It's okay if your trauma has changed you.

Chapter 6

Struggling with Self Image and Worth

A previous chapter talked about validity and shame, and I believe that does tie into this chapter as well. Figuring out who you are after a trauma is hard.

I've mentioned this before, but I'm going to repeat it. You do not have to be who you were before trauma. In fact, you'll probably exhaust yourself trying to be that person. It's okay to be different.

It isn't uncommon for survivors to suffer from low self-esteem after a trauma. Quite a few survivors have difficulty seeing their reflection. For some, it makes them feel sick or ashamed. For others, it can make them feel like they aren't real. A sense of dissociation. *Is that really me? Who is that person?*

In my personal experience, I've had difficulty looking in the mirror ever since I was younger. A part of it comes from me feeling disgusted with myself, but also I struggle with not being able to connect with the girl I'm seeing. I dissociate and constantly ask myself, *is that me? Is that who I am?*

It's taken a long time for me to deal with this, and after a great deal of progress, I was raped as an adult. For me, this set me right back. The morning after the rape, I found myself looking into the mirror in disbelief. I didn't feel like I existed. It was as if I was in some sort of dream. In the weeks that followed, that feeling was slowly replaced with disgust.

I've made progress again and have begun working on my self-image and self-esteem. It hasn't been an easy progress, but I take it day by day.

Trauma has a way of making some individuals feel worthless. It can make them feel dirty or like there's something wrong with them. None of this is true, but unfortunately, it's not as simple as hearing that.

After the sexual abuse I experienced as a child, I had a lot of difficulty with my self-image and worth throughout my teenage years. I was very insecure and this showed in everything I did. I was hesitant to participate in any activities because I was fearful of people looking at me. I'd let myself be walked all over because I thought I deserved it.

It's just been over the last few years I've started to face this head on. The rape as an adult seemed to shatter most of the progress I'd made. Initially, I'd been reluctant to tell people what had happened out of fear they wouldn't believe me due to the fact I was overweight and I considered myself ugly. I know, and I knew then, that rape has nothing to do with appearance but it was still a fear that sat with me.

While I've been working on it, there are still bad days. I find that times I take a lot of care and time in trying to look nice are the times I get the most frustrated. I'll find myself wondering why bother? This usually leads to me not bothering to try due to the discouragement I experience.

For a lot of survivors, myself included, your body may not feel like your own anymore. When I was raped, I had no control. It was as if he'd taken my body and made it his.

One of the more difficult parts was remembering everything he'd said to me. Despite what most may think, it wasn't all bad. He told me I was beautiful. The compliments he gave me feel tainted in a way. It makes compliments today challenging to believe as often I'm brought back to his voice. He made me feel good about myself and played on my trust. He gave me compliments and praises weeks before the rape. It's very hard to believe compliments from anyone because I associate certain compliments with him now and hearing them makes me feel gross. They can also make me feel wrong and like my body isn't mine.

This last part of the chapter includes submissions from other survivors and their experiences with self-image and worth.

For several years of my childhood, I was told every day that I was not enough. That I was worthless. That I didn't deserve love. That even my own family couldn't love me. That I deserved to be hurt. That I was stupid.

Sometimes, I was told this with words. Usually, I was told this with actions. I was told this with punches, kicks, shoves, bites, and chokeholds. Whether it was by words or by actions, the message was always clear.

Logically, I know this wasn't true. I know that I am loved and lovable. I know that I didn't deserve to be beaten the way I was. I know I didn't deserve to be abused.

But I can't really understand that. I can't really accept that in my heart.

I struggle to accept any compliment because I don't believe I deserve it. It's easier to believe what I was told over and over again all those years ago: I'm worthless.

- *Anonymous*

I'm not going to go into detail about what happened. What I will say is it happened for four years.

During these four years I was very young, four to eight years old. At the time I didn't realize just how bad 'it' was and that 'it' shouldn't be happening. What I did realize however was that it felt good so I encouraged it and wanted it and played along.

When I got older, that realization was the worst thing in my life. It made me sick to think about. I hated it. It made me feel guilty and disgusting. It turned into me feeling like all I was good for was being a toy. An object of sexual attention. Along with the feelings of worthlessness, I began to hate my body. I ended up eating to gain weight, thinking that it happened because of how I looked. Along with the weight gain I started to hate being female. I wanted to be a boy just like all my friends because when you're young no one tells you that it happens to boys too. (Especially when I was growing up.)

Right now in my life, I once again hate my body. I hate my weight and my physical features. I feel unattractive and disgusting. I keep saying how much I wish I was little again just so I can fix my weight. To this day I only feel worthwhile when I'm the subject of sexual desire. I'm on the verge of becoming a sex worker because I don't like I can succeed in any other line of work and I want the attention.

I'm stuck in a vicious cycle of self-hatred.

- *Mystery*

It's taken a long time to get to the point where I am realizing I am worthy. I know it's hard, but you have to stop and remind yourself that you are worthy, too. You didn't deserve what happened to you.

What someone else did to you is not your fault. That's a reflection of them and not a reflection of you.

I've learned this about myself. I shouldn't feel dirty because of what they did to me. That is something that speaks about their character and not mine. My worth isn't dependent on someone else and their actions. I am worthy because I am me. The same rule applies to you. The fact that you survived what you did is amazing, and you deserve more credit for that. Please, trust me when I tell you that you are worth so much more than you give yourself credit for.

I'm brought back to something I've said a couple times already. Would you ever tell another survivor the negative things you say to yourself?

I assume and hope that the answer is no. Give yourself the same respect and understanding that you give everyone else.

Chapter 7

Guilt

Despite being right in the title of this book, guilt isn't something I've really talked about yet. However, it is one of the most important parts for me.

Guilt is something I struggle with every day. It's not just about feeling ashamed and guilty for what happened to me, though that is a huge part of it. I also feel a lot of guilt for not reporting the sexual abuse as a child when it was happening.

As I said before, I never told my parents until over a year after the abuse had stopped. There are a number of reasons for this but none alleviate the guilt I feel. The man responsible did tell me that my parents would no longer love me, and that it was my fault. He made me feel like I was doing something wrong. I was scared I would get in trouble if I told my parents.

I always felt dirty. I always felt anxious and I start to shut down as a child.

There are a lot of instances where I wish I'd said something. Any number of times when I could have told my parents. My relationship with my parents had always been stable, but I was so afraid. I have a lot of regret. I wish I'd told my parents the day after the first time. The first time, the man didn't even know I'd woken up. He hadn't had time to threaten me yet. This is the time I come back to the most.

Please note: the next paragraph will be descriptive and potentially trigger. Please skip it if this isn't something you're ready to read.

He'd tickled my feet and I'd pretended to sleep. I continued to pretend I was asleep the entire time. From him removing his pants to him taking my hand. I'd felt anxious when he had forbidden me from sleeping down the hall like I usually did. I didn't understand what was happening, but I was terrified. I was scared if I showed him I was awake I'd get in trouble because, despite not understanding, it felt wrong. I had no comprehension of what I was touching, and I opened my eyes quickly. I remember the confusion. I remember thinking, *doesn't he pee from there?* I was a young child at the time.

This is the event I come back to. He'd thought I was asleep, and therefore, he'd felt no need to warn me not to say anything. The next day, I didn't breathe a word of it to my parents. I felt embarrassed and I didn't know why. If I'd said something then, it would have never happened again.

But I didn't say anything.

This continued on for years. It escalated as time went by. He got braver. I remember thinking if I showed him I was awake one time then he wouldn't do anything. I was wrong. By this point, it stopped mattering to him whether I knew and it was at this point he told me it was my fault. He told me a lot of nasty things that seemed to confirm what I'd already been feeling in my head. That it wasn't okay and there was something wrong with me. He told me that my parents wouldn't love me. This, along with the abuse, contributed to the low self-esteem I would suffer from for years. In my head, I wasn't lovable. I wasn't worthy.

He made me feel ashamed and terrified of anyone finding out which worked in his benefit. I kept my mouth shut. I hid it from my parents because of the fear that they wouldn't love me anymore. I felt like I was doing something wrong, and in a way, felt like I deserved it.

I go back to that first time, almost every day. What if I told my parents then? I know, for a fact, that it would have never happened again.

I think the hardest part for me is that I didn't say anything, and he went on to do it to other children. I feel like maybe I could have prevented that. I know that's not on me. It's not my fault, but the guilt I feel is extreme.

It's not just the first time I go back to, it's just the one I go back to most. I also go back to each time it escalated. When he started touching me. When he started removing my clothes or having me do it. I realize those were all times I could have said something.

One of the times that gets me most is when he raped me. It took years of touching and grooming to get to this point. I was 11 when he raped me. It was then that I realized I couldn't take it anymore. I was in so much pain and I remember having to go to swimming class the next day and I felt like I was burning. That was the day I got back from swimming, gathered my things, and ran away. It never occurred to me to tell my parents. He had me so convinced they would be angry with me. That they wouldn't love me. I realize now that isn't rational, but he'd spent years convincing me of this. In order to make it stop, I ran away.

Even when my parents found me that night, I still didn't tell them. I remember the man that had molested me crying when I got out of the truck. Now I'm sure it was his fear that caused that reaction. He knew why I'd run away and was terrified this would be when I told my parents.

They asked me and pleaded to know why I'd run away. I told them I just 'felt like it,' and that 'I was bored.' I'm sure they knew I was lying but there wasn't anything they could say or do to get the truth out of me.

I feel a lot of guilt for how long it took me to tell my parents. By then, he'd been gone over a year. They took me to the police station that night. I withheld details from the police because I was still terrified. Since I was so reluctant to divulge anything, there was a severe lack of information. The police did what they could, but ultimately, nothing came of it. It was approximately two years later I heard he was being charged for doing it to others. The guilt I felt over that is still something I deal with to this day. I constantly tell myself that he should be the only one feeling guilty, but it doesn't change how I feel. In all honesty, if another survivor told me they felt guilt for not reporting, I would never think they should feel guilty. I'd tell them it wasn't their fault. This seems to be something specific to me. I'm learning to give myself the same respect and understanding I give others. I hope you can, too. I'm sure there are many of you in the same boat as me. It's something we all need to work on together, because we all deserve the same respect and understanding.

I have a lot of guilt about the rape I experienced in adulthood as well. I felt uncomfortable with the guy after I'd told him I wasn't interested. We were in my truck and I was starting to panic. I messaged a friend, and he called me to see if I was okay. I told him I was because I was convinced I was overreacting and not in any danger. I felt uncomfortable, but I pawned it off on previous trauma. I go back to then as well. If I had told my friend I was scared, would it have prevented it? If I had fought more, would the guy have given up? I know I screamed, but what if I'd screamed more?

I'm the first to tell others that it's not healthy to wonder 'what ifs.' I believe that's true. What's done is done, and wondering about what if does nothing to help. It contributes to the feelings of guilt. However, it's a lot easier said than done.

This draws back on acceptance. I've been working at it a long time. Maybe if I had reported my childhood abuser, he wouldn't have been able to do it to others. Maybe that's true, but there's nothing I can do about it now. Wondering 'what if' just hurts me. I'm starting to realize that there's no changing what happened in the past. I got dealt a bad hand and I can't change that. All I can do is work with the now. I can work on myself and work towards a better future. One step at a time.

Guilt is a very common feeling that a lot of survivors have to deal with. Here are some submissions from other survivors about guilt they've dealt with.

Most of my life I went without knowing about my trauma. It didn't seem real to me, I don't know if that's from the fight or flight response or if it was because I could have done more to stop it so it was automatically my fault. I was young and I didn't know any better. I told him no at first, but he kept insisting and eventually he forced himself on to me and I didn't know I was supposed to say no at that point. I felt so ashamed when I grew up and realized what I had done, or hadn't done. I still struggle with feeling guilty about everything that happened within those 3 months, so I have to keep reminding myself that trauma is NEVER the survivors fault. Even if I could have done more, I was only 6 and I didn't know any better.

- Morgan (19)

Guilt and shame are ultimately why I never

really speak about my trauma. I don't believe that should be the case. I think it's important to talk about it because it lets other survivors know that they shouldn't feel guilty or ashamed.

In all honesty, this chapter was the most difficult for me to write. Which leads me to believe it's one of the most important pieces.

If you're like me, and struggling with guilt, I hope that one day you can accept that it wasn't your fault. You survived. Maybe surviving wasn't pretty. In fact, it was probably messy. But you survived. For that, you should be proud.

Chapter 8

Boundaries

Having and establishing boundaries is okay and is a very healthy step for trauma survivors. As hard as it is to say no, you have the right.

"PLEASE, DON'T TOUCH ME"

This is a phrase I find myself thinking frequently.

I don't say it much anymore. Mostly because people have made me feel bad about it. They've made me feel bad for having boundaries about my body and that isn't okay.

Sometimes, they treat it as a joke. I ask them not to touch me and suddenly they're laughing and poking me. "Like that?"

Yes. Like that. And it isn't funny.

When I ask someone not to touch me, it isn't anything personal and yet... most take it that way.

Sometimes they treat me like I'm a child and they tell me to quit being ridiculous.

71

More often than not, I've been told "I'm not hurting you."

I'm very aware you're not hurting me but you need to understand that there was a time when I told someone to stop and they didn't. There was a time when I begged someone to get their hands off of me and they didn't. I told them no and they still thought they had the right.

I'm a rape survivor. I'm also a survivor of childhood sexual abuse. It's taken me a long time to find my voice to express these boundaries.

Trust me when I tell you that I feel guilty when I ask someone not to touch me. I shouldn't have to, but I do. I try and force myself to stay quiet. I make myself uncomfortable trying to protect someone else's feelings. That should not be the way it is.

If I ask someone not to touch me... It isn't personal. It isn't a joke. I'm not being rude. I'm setting a boundary which is something I've struggled to do. People should respect it.

There are many reasons a person may not want to be touched. It doesn't matter what those reasons are.

You have the right to tell someone no. It doesn't matter what it is. A lot of people expect handshakes. Some people expect hugs, or someone may go to pat you reassuringly. You are allowed to tell someone, "I'm not comfortable with you touching me. Please don't. Whether they are family, a co-worker, friend or stranger. You are not being rude. You are using your voice and I think that's a very important and healthy step.

A lot of us had our voice taken away from us. It can be very difficult to find that voice. Especially when people get offended or make you feel embarrassed for rejecting a hug.

I know it's hard, but you have every right to establish boundaries. It's taken me a long time but I have set boundaries with my friends. There are certain people that are allowed to hug me without warning me, but some of them know they need to ask first.

In my case, it's usually as simple as asking permission. When someone stops and says, "is it okay if I hug you?" I'll usually say yes because I feel I have the control over my body which is crucial for me.

I wish it was the norm for people to ask permission before invading your space or putting their hands on you in any way. Unfortunately, this doesn't seem to be the case.

I encourage you all to think about what boundaries you'd like to establish and work your way up to enforcing those. I know it's hard, but try not to feel guilty. It is your right.

Whether it's something like asking your doctor or another health professional to warn you before touching you, or telling your friends you'd appreciate being asked before being touched. It is okay. You aren't being rude. There's nothing wrong with you. Even if your rule is to not be touched in any way, at all, you aren't being unreasonable or a burden. That is okay, and I hope that you don't feel guilty for that.

Some people may be offended, and this is unfortunate. However, I'd rather they be offended than you have to endure feeling uncomfortable, anxious or scared.

Some people may not respect your boundaries. I strongly encourage you, if you can, to cut these people out. I know that isn't always possible, but if it is, please respect yourself as they aren't doing it. If your friend laughs at you and proceeds to cross that boundary, they aren't a friend to you I'm sorry to say.

I've focused a lot on boundaries involving touch and personal space. I want you to know that you can set any boundaries you want. If certain actions or behaviours cause you discomfort, it is okay to set those boundaries too.

I've had to set a few boundaries with 'friends' that only seem to communicate with me when they're in need of a favour. I've set boundaries with people that only use me as their sounding board or free 'therapist.' It gets exhausting taking on everyone's problems and you aren't obligated. If you aren't in a good place yourself, feeling drained or just don't want to help someone, you do not have to. The word "no" is something you're allowed to use.

You don't have to give someone a reason. You don't have to try and explain yourself and make a viable excuse. If it makes you feel better to start out, finding an excuse or explanation may be important to you. I just want you to know that no one is entitled to a reason. Being told "no" should be enough, and if they don't respect that, they aren't someone you want around I'm sorry to say.

You have a voice and you have the right to use that voice. I know and understand the fear of using that voice, but I encourage you to find yours. It took me a long time to find mine, and I feel more in control now. It's crucial to me and has helped me in so many uncomfortable situations.

As usual, I'm going to include some submissions from other survivors in regards to their experiences with boundaries.

My family is extremely "huggy." We hug to greet, say bye, when we're happy, sad, anything. After being raped, I feel like I can't be one of the family anymore. Hugging makes me feel like I can't breathe or I even imagine my family member hurting me. But I hate for them to think I don't trust them anymore. It may be true that I don't trust them as much, but I don't want them to know that. So I stiffly let it happen. I wish I had the strength to tell them I don't want to hug anymore.

- Ashley (NC)

I thought when I got older I would find "the right one" and everything would be rainbows and sunshine. Boy was I wrong. Every relationship I had was forced. I never had any feelings in the relationship or even really had the courage to say no when they asked me to have sex. Even if I desperately wanted to run screaming out of the room from being so uncomfortable. Trauma makes you put yourself through more trauma because it feels "normal" I think that's probably the worst part.

- *Anonymous*

It is so important to set boundaries, especially in situations similar to what happened, in order to not trigger you. E.g: I got into my first relationship not a too long time after being raped. Physical contact is really tough for me, which means that I have to make it clear whenever something becomes too much; my boyfriend is really supportive, but if somebody doesn't respect boundaries, let them go. They wouldn't do you any good and hinder your recovery.

- *Anonymous*

Chapter 9

How Do You Cope?

There's no magic fix. Unfortunately, we all know this. However, when it's difficult, sometimes there are things that may help get through the moment. I've spoken to numerous survivors about the things they do when it's hard. Whether they're having flashbacks or an emotional day. They've told me about all the self-care things they do to get through the rough patches.

I'm going to share some of these with you, and I hope there's something that helps you too. Please keep in mind that none of these are permanent solutions, merely suggestions to get through the bad days.

When it comes to coping with specific things like flashbacks or panic attacks, I've found grounding exercises help. There are various ones to try, and I encourage you to research some. These exercises may help you ground yourself in that moment and help you calm down. Please don't feel ashamed about needing these. There is nothing wrong with you and you aren't weak.

I know it sounds cliché, but there are quite a few breathing exercises I use. Particularly in moments where I feel I'm losing control of my emotions. I used to read or hear about them and laugh them off because it sounded ridiculous. I've since decided to give them a try and I admit I was wrong. Something as simple as focusing on my breathing has helped me numerous times at work. It's also helped me in situations of anger and helped prevent me from saying or doing something I may regret later. I can't promise they will help everyone, but if you're hesitant like I was, I encourage you to look into the various exercises and take a leap of faith. It might be something that helps you out of bad spots like it has me. I hope so.

The next one isn't specific to a mood or situation but is something I've been trying to do lately, and it does seem to help. I find that a lot of the time, my emotional outbursts come from holding everything in. I find the best thing to do for me a lot of the time is to cry it out. I don't try and fight it, I just allow myself to cry. It's a release most of the time, and I tend to feel better afterwards. I'm sure many of you are like me and try and hold it in. My advice is don't. Let it out. Maybe you don't need to cry, but instead, scream. If you need to be quiet, I encourage you to scream into a pillow. It might sound silly, but it really can help you release all the emotions you've pent up during the day.

Another thing I do, and it may seem small but it really does help me calm down, is I'll make myself a warm cup of tea and run myself a bubble bath. Sometimes it's the small things that help the most.

On this note, doing one of your favourite activities is a good distraction as well for a bad day. Whether this is singing, dancing, drawing, reading, playing games or baking.

Please don't forget that there are hotlines available if it's especially rough. Don't be ashamed to reach out. There's no shame in admitting you need help. It doesn't make you weak. We all need help now and again. This is okay. You aren't a burden.

In all honesty, as hard as it is, one of the more helpful things I've found is writing about it. Whether it's poetry, a journal or some other form of writing. Writing about it helps me get my emotions out on paper and helps me come to terms with what happened. This, to me, is a huge part of admitting it.

I've even written letters to my rapist, and the man who molested me during my childhood. I've never sent these, but just writing the letters helped me admit what had happened. It truly felt like a weight had been lifted off my shoulders. It was freeing in a way, and if you are ready, I encourage you to write a letter to of what you wish you could say to them. It's not necessary to send it, but if that is something you wish to do, I fully support you.

For me, writing this book has helped me tremendously. I feel lighter. I find that I can smile and experience genuine joy again. The pain is still there, but I've come so far. Whether writing is something you do already or aren't into, I believe you may find healing in it. I believe that you may find out things about yourself and see things differently. It helped me face a lot and come to terms with what had happened to me.

The most helpful thing for me was finding others that, on some level, understood what I was going through. More often than not, friends and family were willing to be there. However, sometimes you just need to talk to someone that gets it. Finding other trauma survivors was crucial in my coping. That's a part of the reason I've written this book.

As sad as it is that so many have experienced trauma of some sort, it's comforting to know you're not alone. Having someone that understands is one of the most reassuring things. Realizing I wasn't the only one that felt a certain way helped me grasp there wasn't anything wrong with me. Just because no one talked about certain parts of trauma didn't mean I was weird or wrong for experiencing those things. The truth was that a lot of others experienced them as well, but due to stigma and other various reasons, they didn't talk about them either.

That was the goal of this book, and I hope it's helped you to realize that you aren't alone. That being said, I encourage you to find others that understand. A lot of places have support groups, but I understand the anxiety that may give some of you. I also recognize a lot of smaller towns won't have access to these groups. I've found great comfort in online communities as well. The idea of this book started in an online community I am a part of. I threw the idea out there about writing a book that was meant to help validate and make survivors feel they weren't alone. I received a lot of encouragement, and here we are.

These next few are suggestions sent into me by fellow survivors.

On really bad days, I put on my running shoes and go for a brisk walk around the nature preserve at my university. Personally, being close to nature makes me feel more grounded. I bring my iPod and blast tunes so loud that they drown out all of my thoughts. After the walk, I take a nice, warm shower to help me relax. I then usually treat myself to some ice cream, as a kind of reward for getting through the bad times. It isn't always easy, but it helps.

- *Jennifer, Miami FL, 21*

For me, I would go for a car ride or a walk. I would crank my music as loud as I could. I was fortunate enough and am fortunate enough to live close to the ocean and I would always make a point of going to the beach when nobody else was around. Just listening to the waves. Always worked for me to the point where I was always shocked to see how much time had actually passed. It always made me feel better. It would give me a sense of freedom and control.

- *Anonymous*

The way I cope is by cuddling with my fur babies. They make me feel so loved and secure. Whenever I have a bad day, holding my fur babies makes everything seem better. They give me a reason to try and go on.

- *Anonymous*

Personally, I've also found comfort in reading about the experiences of other survivors. Once again, this helped me not feel alone. This is why the next chapter includes poetry submitted to me by other survivors.

I hope that you can find some comfort in it as well, but please be aware some of the poems may be descriptive in ways that may be triggering. Please only read these poems if it's something you feel you are in a state to handle at the moment.

Chapter 10

Poetry Submissions

This entire chapter consists of poetry submissions sent in by other survivors about their experience.

NEVER FORGET BY ALEXANA CARTER

Never forget the pain,
Tears forming,
Skin turning purple,
Yelps escaping
Fists pounding
Over and over
Against the body.

Never forget the lies,
Excuses for bruises,
Eye rolls once again,
Punishments for truth,
Whispered threats
Crying at night
After pleas for help.

Never forget rising
From the ashes,

Wings ablaze,
Stronger than ever,
Unbreakable,
Unstoppable,

A whole new being.

AND I LIKE IT BY EMMETT - THE BALLAD OF SEXUAL DEPENDENCY (INSPIRED BY NAN GOLDIN)

she told me she loved me.
and I believed her.
her calloused hands felt so good on my body,
they explored every crevasse, every mole, every
freckle,
the curves of my breasts and my stomach and my hips,
the edges of my bones,
and the softness of my skin.
and I liked it.

her salt laced lips pressed into me,
my neck,
my shoulders,
my back,
my everything.
she planted a trail of kisses down my body,
her lips touching every square inch,
it's as if she were trying to memorize how I felt
beneath her.
and I liked it.

I liked the way she held me,
and the way she whispered in my ear,
the way she called me "sweetheart", "babe",
"honey",
the way she said my name.

her limbs knotted with mine
and we were tied together,
laughing,
smiling,
holding each other.
and I liked it.

her voice was soft, and rumbly, and deep.
every word she spoke was an earthquake,
and her tongue was a tremor.
it tilted in my mouth,
twirling perfectly with mine.
her beard rubbed against my cheek,
making goosebumps leap from under my skin,
and I liked it.
And I liked it until I didn't like it anymore.

SOMETHING'S MISSING BY APRIL

I can see my pink nightgown,
Tossed to the side.
I long to be back in it
And not under you.

"Shh, it's our little secret."
The blood is gushing out of my nose.
Like when that basketball hit me in the face.

I remember you cleaning me up after that incident.
Will you clean me up this time?
Even if it was your hand that caused it,
in a quick desperation to silence my cries?

The basketball.
That day is so vivid.
I can even feel the warm air on my face.
Or is that your breath?

There's more blood now.
Except it's coming from somewhere else.
I have no memory to compare this one too.
No memory to escape to the past from the present.

A dish shatters.

Just like me.

She's in the kitchen.
Your whispers are so loud.
Surely she must hear them.

The rush of footsteps never come.
The door is never thrown open.
No one comes to save me.

It's just me.
And you.
Your body.
My body.

Is it still mine?
Haven't you made it yours?

It's over.
Something's missing.
I find my way back inside the pink nightgown.
But something's still missing.

STOCKHOLM BY A.D

a harsh blow to the nape of the neck and i am
composed
sympathetic stimulation protects me from the pain
of this r e v e r s e empathy

you took away all that i would need
so when the time came to give in
my spine would surrender with little coercion
(you did it so calmly and softly that i even thanked
you for it)

untouched, sterile and nobody s a i d   a n y t h i n g

nothing, no
the teddy bear peignoir drenched in semen
and the divine voices in my head telling me to burn it
but i needed to feel you / i need
you

all i fucking have left
is weak clitoral sensation and
a mistrust of anyone's grip on me

i walk as if i can leave my body behind
but this heavy armour hangs from my feeble form
and my bones are sore; painfully unveiled and
protruding

even when i'm (un)safely wrapped in warm, silk sheets
it hurts as much as it did that day

we communicated only through nursery rhymes
to protect you from the growing pains of maturity
your spirit: too quaint to belong to a man
who were you? a boy encased in adult lies

i try to imagine you with the burdens i have
and so you appear to me as a guilt-ridden, violent mass
of transparent enamel and bleeding gums

you are unsightly in my subconscious
and no longer will i suckle like an infant
on the bosom of your ego

FLASHBACK BY LISA

I get aches in my stomach...
Tears in my eyes...

I close them and I am thrown back...

Lying there...
Suffocated from tears...
Helpless...
Breathless...

Counting ducks on the lampshade...

7!

It's 7!

Yellow, with orange beaks.

They are looking at me.
They see everything.
But they keep silence.

Like me.

'Shhhhh... it's our secret...' he whispers.
A secret that is like a hidden treasure.

I will keep my promise.

Like the ducks do.

UNTITLED BY K.E.G.

I tried to wash you from my body. I scrubbed and scrubbed past the point of feeling clean, until my skin broke and tiny droplets of crimson shined before me and silently fell to the shower floor.

I tried to cleanse my body of you.

I tried to rinse away the filthy feeling and scent of you. I doused myself in every soap I could find, until my skin burned from the chemicals that now lost their aroma.

I tried to remove you from me,

From my skin,

My nails,

My hair,

My mind,

But when I looked in the mirror all I could see was you.

All I could feel was your hands on my skin, tracing hearts along my thighs, how dare you tell me, everything will be alright.

I screamed and screamed until it felt like my lungs would bleed, praying it would silence my mind from you. But you were still there. You held me down, and whispered, burning, choking, nothings into my ears.

I tried to burn you from every fabric I owned, watching as the colors and threads turned to a silent snowfall of ashes.

But. You. Were. Still. There.

Embroidered on my favorite sweater, it would no longer feel safe and warm, blanketing me from the burning, stinging, vicious and unforgiving cold of winter, that was your touch.

And most of all, I tried to kill you. With every cigarette and every sip of whiskey, I prayed it would drown you mercilessly, begging for air like I begged for my innocence. Until I realized, you were not something that could be killed.

You are the blood on my skin, and the screaming in my brain. You are the poison the drags me into the nightmare and the hell that sleep is. You are not human enough to be killed. You were not human enough to own my body, nor will you ever be.

Epilogue

A lot of trauma survivors find themselves struggling with who they are after trauma. We've touched on this, but I'd like to go into it a little bit more.

Trauma is messy and awful. There's no argument about that. I've discussed how I dislike how society pushes the beautiful survivor trope on us. It can leave a lot of survivors feeling like they're doing something wrong or weak because they aren't where society thinks they should be. I fully support all survivors, and don't believe they have to come out better or kind. However, this isn't to say that you can't. For some, making good come out of what they went through is how they cope. If this isn't you, that's completely okay. There's nothing wrong with you if you don't have any goal and anyone that tells you that you need to "find the silver lining" is wrong. How you deal is ultimately up to you.

What you went through will never be okay, however, you can take your power back.

Whether you've made it through the book or just came to the end because you needed it, I'm so glad you're reading this.

I wish it didn't have to come to an end because I feel there's still so much to say but it'll never all fit in a book. I've done my best to cover what I feel is important, but I know there's a lot left unsaid.

I want to end with something important. Probably the most important part. So, please, read this next bit and take it in because I mean every word. It doesn't matter who you are. This applies to **you.**

You are worthy. You are worth so much more than you could possibly think. You deserve respect and understanding and did not deserve what happened to you. What you went through was wrong, and I wish there was something I could do to change it.

Unfortunately, I can't. What I will tell you is you aren't alone. Whatever your trauma, you are valid. No matter the circumstances, it wasn't your fault. No one had the right to do what was done to you.

I know it's hard and scary at times. I know how difficult the struggle can be but I want to tell you that it'll be okay. I truly believe that.

You shouldn't be ashamed. You survived and continue to do so and I am so proud of every single one of you.

No matter how hard it gets, please remember you aren't alone. We're all in this together.

Made in the USA
Las Vegas, NV
15 November 2020